GUIDED READING NOTES

Dark Blue Band
Oxford Level 16

GRAPHIC TEXTS

Contents

Introduction	2
The Sands of Deception (Character fiction)	8
The Secret Garden (Classic)	16
I Wandered Lonely as a Cloud *and other poems* (Poetry)	24
Great Naturalists (Non-fiction)	33

OXFORD
UNIVERSITY PRESS

Introduction

Why is guided reading important?

Guided reading plays an important role in your whole-school provision for reading, providing opportunities for children to progress and develop the key competencies they need to become confident and skilled independent readers. Working with small groups of children, with texts closely matched to the readers' needs, guided reading is the perfect vehicle for delivering focused teaching from Reception/PI right through to Year 6/P7. The teacher-pupil interaction also provides a valuable assessment opportunity, helping you identify exactly what each child can and can't do. Through guided reading children also encounter a world of exciting, whole books – building a community of readers who read for pleasure.

About *Project X Origins*

Project X Origins is a comprehensive, whole-school guided reading programme designed to help you teach the wide range of skills essential to ensure children progress as readers and to help nurture a love of reading.

Ensuring the key skills are covered

Project X Origins incorporates all of the key skills children need to develop to become successful and enthusiastic readers:

> **Word reading:** phonically regular and common exception words are introduced systematically in the early levels with phonic opportunities provided throughout the notes. As children progress, they are encouraged to use their decoding skills whenever they encounter new or unfamiliar words, and also to recognize how this impacts on different spelling rules.

> **Comprehension:** understanding what has been read is central to being an effective and engaged reader but comprehension is not something that comes automatically so specific strategies have been built into the notes to ensure children develop comprehension skills they can use over a range of texts:

- Previewing
- Predicting
- Activating and building prior knowledge
- Questioning
- Recalling
- Visualizing and other sensory responses
- Deducting, inferring and drawing conclusions
- Determining importance
- Synthesizing
- Empathizing
- Summarizing
- Personal response, including adopting a critical response

> **Reading fluency:** fluency occurs as children develop automatic word recognition, reading with pace and expression. Strategies to help achieve this, including meaningful opportunities for oral reading, rereading and re-listening are provided throughout.

> **Vocabulary:** introducing new vocabulary within a meaningful context is an important element in extending children's vocabulary range, developing their reading fluency and comprehension. *Project X Origins Graphic Texts* provides opportunities in every book for learning new and higher-level vocabulary in context, with the support of detailed illustrations.

> **Grammar, punctuation and spelling:** learning about language in the context of a text, rather than through a series of discrete exercises, can help make grammar, punctuation and spelling relevant and helps children make the link between grammar, punctuation and clarity of meaning, thus supporting their development as writers. Opportunities to support an in-depth look at language are provided for every book.

> **Spoken language:** talk is crucial to learning and developing their comprehension so children are given plenty of opportunities to: discuss and debate their ideas with others; justify their opinions; ask and answer questions; explore and hypothesize; summarize, describe and explain; and listen and respond to the ideas of others.

Assessment and progression in reading

Project X Origins includes a rigorous assessment spine drawn from the *Oxford Reading Criterion Scale* to ensure that you know exactly what each child can do and what they need to focus on next in order to make progress. This assessment framework, combined with the careful levelling of the Oxford Levels, will help you select the right book with the right level of challenge for each of your guided reading groups and to assess, track and monitor each child's progress.

Step 1

On a termly basis, use the *Oxford Reading Criterion Scale* (which can be found in the *Project X Origins Graphic Texts Teaching Handbook Years 4–6 (P5–7)*) to assess each child's reading. The scale will tell you the Oxford Level a child is comfortable reading at and the areas a child needs to develop. You can also use this assessment to form your guided reading groups.

Step 2

Plan your guided reading sessions by selecting books at the appropriate Oxford Level that focus on the relevant learning needs of the group. You will find charts showing the learning objectives and assessment points for every graphic text in the *Project X Origins Graphic Texts Teaching Handbook Years 4–6 (P5–7)*. Depending on your assessment, you might choose a book at the level the children are comfortable at or one from the next level up, to offer some stretch.

Step 3

Use the assessment points within the Guided Reading Notes to support on-going assessment of children's reading progress. The Progress Tracking Charts in the *Project X Origins Graphic Texts Teaching Handbook Years 4–6 (P5–7)* can be used to record this if you wish. Regularly re-assess each child's progress combining your on-going informal assessments and the termly assessment using the *Oxford Reading Criterion Scale*. Use this information to re-organize guided reading groups and teaching plans in response to children's varying degrees of progress.

Getting started: using the Guided Reading Notes

At a glance
Project X Origins Guided Reading Notes offer detailed guidance to help deliver effective and engaging guided reading sessions, and are designed to be used flexibly to ensure you get the most out of each book. For notes containing multiple sessions, you may choose to focus on each of these sessions or focus on one session and have the children read the rest of the book independently.

Curricular correlation and assessment
At the beginning of every set of notes there are correlation charts for all UK curricula, ensuring that across the clusters the main curricular objectives are covered. In addition, an overview of assessment points for each book is provided – these points are also signposted throughout the notes. See the *Project X Origins Graphic Texts Teaching Handbook Years 4–6 (P5–7)* for more information.

Key information
Before the first session, an overview of the book and the resources you will need (such as additional photocopy masters) is provided.

Teaching sequence
Each guided reading session follows the same teaching sequence:

- **Before reading**: children explore the context of each book to support their understanding and help them engage with the text. They are encouraged to discuss, recall, respond, predict and speculate about the book. Graphic texts offer a different reading experience and they may take longer to comprehend than other types of books. Therefore it is recommended that reading takes place outside of the guided reading session as far as possible.
- **During reading**: children are given a section of the book to reread with specific questions in mind.
- **After reading**: children reflect on and discuss what they have read. They are encouraged to delve deeper, exploring their understanding of the text, developing their vocabulary, grammar, punctuation, spelling and fluency where appropriate.
- **Follow-up**: opportunities for children to extend their learning outside the session are provided, including writing and cross-curricular activities.

Guided reading with graphic texts

Graphic texts are an incredibly powerful way of developing comprehension skills. A guided reading session with a graphic text can bring out children's interest and enthusiasm but also demonstrate their skills and abilities, perhaps more than any other type of text.

Because of the level of internalizing needed to comprehend a graphic text, it is suggested that you ask the children to read the text/section that you will be studying, prior to the session. In addition, you may want to consider the possible areas for discussion before conducting the session:

Approaching the text

A stimulating way to capture children's interest when first approaching a text together can be to choose a panel that represents a key moment from the story and have children articulate what led to this point and what might ensue.

Cinematic analysis

Consider the point of view the illustrator has brought to certain frames. What is the impact of a close up, a long distance shot, an overhead or an upward-looking angle? What has been put in the foreground/background? How is the scene 'lit'? From which character's viewpoint are we experiencing the scene, or is the scene presented to us as external observers?

Illustration style

Illustrators have different styles; sometimes, a particular illustrator is chosen because their style suits the material; also, some illustrators may adapt their style for different effects. Have children consider the appropriateness of the style to the subject matter or atmosphere.

The palette used by an illustrator is always worth noting: have they gone for realism, hyper-realism, romantic, or sombre and subdued? Sometimes stark changes in colouring may indicate turning points in a story, shifts in mood, or transitions in location or time, or one point of view to another.

Changes in time

Graphic texts can have a distinctive way of playing with time; for example, through narrative inserts containing adverbials, such as, 'Later …' or the leaping of time and place from one frame to the next. It is worth investigating this. How much time has passed? How much space has been covered? What's the duration of, say, a single page? The same number of panels can represent seconds, minutes, weeks or decades, so compare how time passes on different pages. And, where they occur, how have any flashbacks been signalled, stylistically?

What happens between panels
Notice what isn't said and what isn't depicted, especially between panels. There is often much to be inferred in the transitions.

Sub-plots
In more complex stories, look out for how sub-plots complement the main story and how they are handled so that a reader doesn't become confused by events running alongside each other. Why does the sub-plot matter? What would happen if it were removed?

Characters
Look closely at what characters say, the specific words they use and the way they say them — the facial expressions and body language represented as well as the point of view. Are the words accompanied with a tear, a smirk or a grimace?

Viewpoint
Notice also the relationship between said dialogue and any narrative inserts; is there some conflict, or different viewpoint, between the narrator and certain characters?

The Sands of Deception
BY ELEN CALDECOTT

Curricular correlation

English National Curriculum

Spoken language	Articulate and justify answers, arguments and opinions
Word reading	Apply their growing knowledge of root words, prefixes and suffixes (etymology and morphology), both to read aloud and to understand the meaning of new words they meet
Comprehension	Check that the book makes sense to them, discussing their understanding and exploring the meaning of words in context
	Draw inferences such as inferring characters' feelings, thoughts and motives from their actions, and justifying inferences with evidence
	Predict what might happen from details stated and implied

Developing grammar, punctuation and spelling

Grammar and Punctuation	Brackets, dashes or commas to indicate parenthesis	Kalvin Spearhead, head of END CO – the most powerful company on Earth – plans to build a giant vortex machine He has assembled a team of human-like robots, Tick-Tock Men, to collect seven Artefacts of Time
Vocabulary and Spelling	Words ending in –able	capable, valuable
	Challenge and context words	sundial, ancestors, particles, apparel, evade, procession, precariously, ventilation, colossal, somersaults, impersonated, immobilize, radically, altered, premises, forbidding, commencing, paralysis, space-time continuum, enveloped, duration, adjusted, archaeologists, revered

Reading assessment points (Oxford Reading Criterion Scale: Assessment Standard 6)

3. Can the children skim and scan to identify key ideas in a text? (R)
5. Can the children explore potential alternatives that could have occurred in texts (e.g. a different ending), referring to text to justify their ideas? (D)
6. Can the children summarize and explain the main points in a text, referring back to the text to support and clarify summaries? (R)
11. Can the children discuss how an author builds a character through dialogue, action and description? (D)
16. Can the children infer and deduce meaning based on evidence drawn from different points in the text? (D)
18. Can the children read between the lines, using clues from action, dialogue and description to interpret meaning and explain how and why characters are acting, thinking or feeling? (D)

Scottish Curriculum for Excellence

Listening and talking	I can show my understanding of what I listen to or watch by responding to literal, inferential, evaluative and other types of questions, and by asking different kinds of questions of my own LIT 2-07a
Reading	To show my understanding across different areas of learning, I can identify and consider the purpose and main ideas of a text and use supporting detail LIT 2-16a
	To show my understanding, I can respond to literal, inferential and evaluative questions and other close reading tasks and can create different kinds of questions of my own ENG 2-17a
	I can discuss structure, characterisation and/or setting; recognise the relevance of the writer's theme and how this relates to my own and others' experiences; discuss the writer's style and other features appropriate to genre ENG 2-19a

Programme of Study for English in Wales

Oracy	Explain information and ideas, exploring and using ways to be convincing, *e.g. use of vocabulary, gesture, visual aids*
Reading	Use a range of strategies to make meaning from words and sentences, including knowledge of phonics, word roots, word families, syntax, text organisation and prior knowledge of context
	Show understanding of main ideas and significant details in texts, *e.g. mindmapping showing hierarchy of ideas, flowchart identifying a process*
	Infer meaning which is not explicitly stated, *e.g. What happens next?, Why did he/she do that?*

Northern Ireland Curriculum

Talking and listening	Describe and talk about real experiences and imaginary situations and about people, places, events and artefacts
Reading	Consider, interpret and discuss texts, exploring the ways in which language can be manipulated in order to affect the reader or engage attention
	Justify their responses logically, by inference, deduction and/or reference to evidence within the text

Session 1 (Chapter 1)

About this book
In this adventure, the micro-friends and Birdy go to Ancient Egypt to protect Pharaoh Seti's sundial – but they arrive at the wrong time and there's something strange about the new pharaoh …

You will need
- *Overcoming obstacles* Photocopy Master, *Graphic Texts Teaching Handbook Years 4–6 (P5–7)*

Before reading
- Recap what can be recalled about the *Project X* characters. **(activating prior knowledge)**
- If they've read other adventures with the micro-friends and Birdy, recap on what they can recall about them; in particular, the hunt for specific artefacts of time from throughout history. **(recall)**
- Read Birdy's story on page 2 and discuss how this helps with memories of the story.

During reading
- Ask the children to read Chapter 1 independently, focussing on the mission, and the particular problems the children face.

After reading
Returning to the text
Ask the children:
- What are the five children looking for? What problem do they face with this? How has this come about? **(recall)**
- What solution does Max suggest to this problem? How does Birdy's knowledge help with this solution?
- How is Tiger feeling in the top-right panel of page 5? How do you know? **(inferring)**
- Why are the children chased? What is their obvious solution?
- Why doesn't this work for Tiger and Birdy?

Assessment point
Can the children summarize and explain the main points in a text, referring back to the text to support and clarify summaries? (ORCS Standard 6, 6)

Developing deeper comprehension

- How might the friends be feeling towards their technology throughout this chapter? What do they use to solve their problems?
- Looking back at page 2, why might Birdy's Escape Wheel cause problems? **(inferring)**
- What can we learn about each character from their actions and reactions in this chapter?
- How might Tiger and Birdy escape from the guard at the beginning of the next chapter? **(predicting)**

Assessment point
Can the children read between the lines, using clues from action, dialogue and description to interpret meaning and explain how and why characters are acting, thinking or feeling? (ORCS Standard 6, 18)

Developing grammar, punctuation and spelling

- Turn back to page 2 and ask the children to find the sentence that uses dashes to indicate parenthesis: *Kalvin Spearhead, head of END CO – the most powerful company on Earth – plans to build a giant vortex machine.*
- Ask them which other punctuation marks could have been used for a similar effect, e.g. brackets or commas, and write the sentence using these marks to confirm this.
- Ask the children to find the word *valuable* on page 4. Is there another way of spelling this word ending (*-ible*)?
- Challenge the children to find or think of at least two more words ending in -ible and two more ending in -able, and check the spellings in the dictionary. Add the words to the children's current list of spellings to be learned.

- Prior to Session 2, ensure children have read Chapters 2 and 3 independently.

Session 2 (Chapters 2 and 3)

Before reading

- Recap the events of Chapters 2 and 3 from independent reading.
- In particular, try to recall the problems the children face, and how they resolve them. **(recall, activating prior knowledge)**

During reading

- Ask the children to reread Chapters 2 and 3 independently.
- Ask them to focus on the perils the two separated groups face, and how these are overcome.
- Ask them also to notice particularly how Birdy and Max respond to problems.

After reading

Returning to the text

Ask the children:

- What dilemma do Max, Cat and Ant face on page 8?
- Why do Max, Cat and Ant choose to follow the pharaoh?
- Why do Birdy and Tiger make the mistake of hiding amongst snakes (p.9)?
- Why does Tiger question Birdy's plan initially? Why does he then decide to go along with it?
- How is Birdy feeling at the bottom of page 12? How might Tiger's question exacerbate this? **(inferring)**
- What do we learn about Ant on page 13?
- What is meant by *micro-landslide*? (p.14) Are the stones colossal? How does the illustration emphasize the sense of danger? **(visualizing)**
- Why does Ant stop Cat from disabling the Tick-Tock Man? (p.17)

Assessment point

Can the children infer and deduce meaning based on evidence drawn from different points in the text? (ORCS Standard 6, 16)

Developing deeper comprehension

- Revisit Ant's plan on page 13: try to explain it in your own words (with the book closed!)
- Look back at the behaviour of Birdy and Max during times of crisis; what do we learn about their respective characters? Ensure that the children understand that these two are the main problem-solvers.
- How do the other three children respond to the plans and ideas from Max and Birdy?

Assessment point

Can the children discuss how an author builds a character through dialogue, action and description? (ORCS Standard 6, 11)

- Prior to Session 3, ensure children have read Chapters 4 and 5 independently.

Session 3 (Chapters 4 and 5)

Before reading
- Recap Chapters 4 and 5 together.
- Again, try to recall the perils the children face and how they escape to continue their mission. **(recall)**

During reading
- Ask the children to reread Chapters 4 and 5 independently.
- Ask them to focus again on any problems that the characters encounter.

After reading
Returning to the text

Ask the children:
- Why does Max think it is necessary to act quickly (p.21)? How are they prevented from acting (p.22)?
- What is so scary about the Tick-Tock Man's weapon based on the fact file on page 23? (What would happen if no-one released you?)
- How do Birdy and Tiger find the pharaoh? What has happened to him? What is he like?
- How do we know Birdy and Tiger are shocked to meet the pharaoh (p.24)? Why are they so surprised? **(drawing conclusions)**
- How does the Pharaoh help them to escape? Then how does he help to defeat the Tick-Tock Man?
- What is important about Tiger's happy statement at the bottom of page 27? What does his facial expression tell us? **(deducing)**
- Why does the Pharaoh give up his sundial p.29)?

Assessment point
Can the children skim and scan to identify key ideas in a text? (ORCS Standard 6, 3)

Developing deeper comprehension

- What is the effect of the inclusion of the fact file page on page 23?
- How does it compare to the information on page 32? What is the key difference? Ensure the children understand that one describes a fictional device and the other, a real historical artefact.
- Why does Birdy bury the sundial, rather than take it with her? Talk about the fact that her mission is to prevent the Tick-Tock Men collecting the artefacts, NOT to collect them herself; also note that she is ensuring that it is in the right place, so that history is not changed. **(questioning, inferring)**
- Return to the entire text and notice together how the artist uses angles and perspective to create atmosphere. Discuss how this reflects the sense of almost constant danger and excitement. **(visualizing)**
- Using the *Overcoming obstacles* Photocopy Master, ask the children to record three problems faced by the children throughout the book, and their respective solutions. Discuss as a group: how else might they have solved these problems? What do the solutions the characters found tell us about them?

Assessment point
Can the children explore potential alternatives that could have occurred in texts (e.g. a different ending), referring to text to justify their ideas? (ORCS Standard 6, 5)

Follow-up

Writing activities

- Choose any of the five characters in this story, and write a diary entry following the events of this adventure. Ensure that your character comments on some of the other children's actions. (**short writing task**)

Other literacy activities

- In a pair or group of three, discuss the five characters and try to decide which has the best leadership skills, and which is the most valuable to the team as a whole. Try to make a case for more than one child in each category.

Cross-curricular activities

- Find out more about the pharaohs Rameses and Seti. Try to find out about their tombs and treasures, and the sundial, too. (**History**)

The Secret Garden
BY FRANCES HODGSON BURNETT
(ADAPTED BY MIRANDA WALKER)

Curricular correlation

English National Curriculum

Spoken language	Use relevant strategies to build their vocabulary
	Consider and evaluate different viewpoints, attending to and building on the contributions of others
Word reading	Apply their growing knowledge of root words, prefixes and suffixes (etymology and morphology), both to read aloud and to understand the meaning of new words they meet
Comprehension	Increase their familiarity with a wide range of books, including myths, legends, and traditional stories, modern fiction, fiction from our literary heritage, and books from other cultures and traditions
	Identify and discuss themes and conventions in and across a wide range of writing
	Check that the book makes sense to them, discussing their understanding and exploring the meaning of words in context
	Draw inferences such as inferring characters' feelings, thoughts and motives from their actions, and justifying inferences with evidence

Developing grammar, punctuation, and spelling

Grammar and Punctuation	Indicating degrees of possibility using **adverbs** [for example, *perhaps, surely*] or **modal verbs** [for example, *might, should, will, must*]	maybe would, can, must, will, could
Vocabulary and Spelling	Words containing the letter-string ough	thought, enough, brought, through, bought
	Challenge and context words	confine, lass, moor, rugged, tamed, intrigued, trepidation, orchard, mite, eluded, wuthering, weathered, steeled, compelled, exquisite, amuse, sow, monsoon, pacified, tranquil, spirits, overwhelmed, blossomed, depicting, erected

Reading assessment points (Oxford Reading Criterion Scale: Assessment Standard 6)

2. Can the children clarify the meaning of unknown words from the way they are used in context? (D)
8. Can the children use inference and deduction skills to discuss messages, moods, feelings and attitudes using the clues from the text? (D)
11. Can the children discuss how an author builds a character through dialogue, action and description? (D)

13.	Can the children discuss how a text may affect the reader and refer back to the text to back up a point of view? (E)
16.	Can the children infer and deduce meaning based on evidence drawn from different points in the text? (D)
18.	Can the children read between the lines, using clues from action, dialogue and description to interpret meaning and explain how and why characters are acting, thinking or feeling? (D)
19.	Can the children justify and elaborate on thoughts, feelings, opinions and predictions, referring back to the text for evidence? (R/D)

Scottish Curriculum for Excellence

Listening and talking	When I engage with others, I can respond in ways appropriate to my role, show that I value others' contributions and use these to build on thinking LIT 2-02a
Reading	I regularly select and read, listen to or watch texts which I enjoy and find interesting, and I can explain why I prefer certain texts and authors LIT 1-11a/LIT 2-11a
	I can select and use a range of strategies and resources before I read, and as I read, to make meaning clear and give reasons for my selection LIT 2-13a
	To show my understanding, I can respond to literal, inferential and evaluative questions and other close reading tasks and can create different kinds of questions of my own ENG 2-17a

Programme of Study for English in Wales

Oracy	Build on and develop the ideas of others in group discussions, *e.g. by asking questions to explore further, offering more ideas*
Reading	Use a range of strategies for skimming, *e.g. finding key words, phrases, gist, main ideas, themes*
	Infer meaning which is not explicitly stated, *e.g. What happens next?, Why did he/she do that?*
	Identify what the writer thinks about the topic, *e.g. admires a historical figure, only interested in facts*

Northern Ireland Curriculum

Talking and listening	Identify and ask appropriate questions to seek information, views and feelings
Reading	Consider, interpret and discuss texts, exploring the ways in which language can be manipulated in order to affect the reader or engage attention
	Use a range of cross-checking strategies to read unfamiliar words in texts

Session I (Chapter I)

About this book

This is a graphic retelling of the classic story about the power of nature to transform people and bring them together.

You will need

- *Changes in Mary* Photocopy Master, *Graphic Texts Teaching Handbook Years 4–6 (P5–7)*

❯ Before reading

- Discuss the title: has anyone read this story in its original form or heard of it? What predictions can be made from the title, if nothing is known about the story? **(predicting)**
- Explain that the original was written in 1911, and describes a way of living that may seem quite strange to us now. One of the focuses for these sessions will be to think about what the story can tell us now in the 21st century.
- Also explain that the main character, Mary, has been living a spoilt but neglected life in India; the story begins as she returns home, following the death of her parents (from cholera).

❯ During reading

- Ask the children to read Chapter 1 independently.
- Ask the children to keep a note of any unfamilar words, e.g. *sour*, *intrigued*, *trepidation*.
- Prompt them to think particularly about the character of Mary. Encourage them to make notes on the *Changes in Mary* Photocopy Master as they read through the book.

❯ After reading

Returning to the text

Ask the children:

- How does Mary feel about her new home, and the moor? How do you know?
- How does Mary regard herself (p.3)?
- What does page 5 tell us about Mary's upbringing in India?
- Why was Mrs Craven's garden locked up? (p.5)

- On pages 6–7, what does Mary want more than anything, and where does she think she'll get this?
- What do we learn about Mrs Medlock from her thoughts, her speech, and her facial expressions? **(inferring)**
- What is Martha's role, and what is her personality? **(deducing)**
- What is special about Martha's brother, Dickon?
- What does the panel at the bottom of page 3 suggest about Mr Craven? **(drawing conclusions)**

> **Assessment point**
> Can the children use inference and deduction skills to discuss messages, moods, feelings and attitudes using the clues from the text? (ORCS Standard 6, 8)

Developing deeper comprehension

- Discuss the overall impression of Mary, with reference to her scenes throughout Chapter 1. Make predictions about how she may change/develop through the rest of the story. How is her life different to 21st-century childhood?
- Ensure the children pick up on the sense of mystery and secrets throughout Chapter 1; ask them to find examples of these elements over the first six pages.
- How does the presentation of nature throughout Chapter 1 contrast with the presentation of the house? Refer to the illustrations as well as the text. **(visualizing)**
- What do we notice about the effect of nature on Mary towards the end of the chapter? **(deducing)**

> **Assessment point**
> Can the children justify and elaborate on thoughts, feelings, opinions and predictions, referring back to the text for evidence? (ORCS Standard 6, 19)

Developing vocabulary

- What unfamiliar words did you find? Can you work out the meanings of the words by looking at the surrounding text? If the meaning's unclear, look the words up in a dictionary. **(deducing)**

> **Assessment point**
> Can the children clarify the meaning of unknown words from the way they are used in context? (ORCS Standard 6, 2)

The Secret Garden

> **Developing grammar, punctuation and spelling**
>
> - Find words in Chapter 1 conveying uncertainty and possibility, e.g. *will*: *Fresh air and play will put colour in them cheeks of yours.* (p. 7). Remind the children that modal verbs appear before the main verb. Can the children see how the word *will* shows possibility?
> - Ask the children, in pairs, to read this sentence aloud, and then change the modal verb, e.g. *Fresh air and play might put colour in them cheeks of yours.*
> - Come together and discuss how the meaning of the sentence changes from one of certainty to uncertainty.
> - Find the word *maybe* on page 6, and discuss how adverbs like *maybe*, *perhaps* and *surely* also help to convey different degrees of certainty.

- Prior to Session 2, ensure children have read Chapters 2 and 3 independently.

Session 2 (Chapters 2 and 3)

Before reading

- Recall and discuss the content of Chapters 2 and 3. **(recall)**
- Try to remember details about the effect of the outdoors on Mary. **(activating prior knowledge)**
- Also try to recall the character of Dickon. **(recall)**

During reading

- Reread Chapters 2 and 3 independently, focussing particularly on how Mary changes.
- Remind the children to consider the effect of the illustrations as well as the story content.

After reading

Returning to the text

Ask the children:

- How does the layout of page 8 help us to understand Mary's gradual change? **(visualizing)**
- How does Mary feel about the secret garden on pages 9–10?

- How is the sense of mystery built up on pages 10–11? What do you predict the crying to be? **(predicting)**
- How does nature appear to help Mary find her way into the secret garden? **(deducing)**
- What is the effect of the illustrations on pages 14–15? **(visualizing)**
- What are Mary's first two reactions on entering the secret garden?
- What is important about the way Dickon is introduced, particularly visually? What does this tell us about him? **(drawing conclusions)**

Assessment point
Can the children infer and deduce meaning based on evidence drawn from different points in the text? (ORCS Standard 6, 16)

Developing deeper comprehension

- How does spending time outdoors change Mary? How does the secret garden enhance this change?
- Mr Craven's property has a secret garden and forbidden rooms; what does this suggest to us? And what is Mary's reaction to both? **(deducing)**
- How would you describe the relationship between Mary and Dickon? Ensure the children understand that he is her first (human) friend, that he is like a teacher to her, and also that he is the only person so far she has shared the secret garden with.
- The penultimate panel on page 19 shows Dickon's and Mary's hands in the soil; what can we infer from this, particularly about Mary? What does this tell us about how she has changed since page 4? **(inferring)**
- How does the last panel on page 19 contrast with Mary's outlook at the beginning of the story? Note the caption text as well as her own statement. **(deducing)**

Assessment point
Can the children discuss how an author builds a character through dialogue, action and description? (ORCS Standard 6, 11)

- Prior to Session 3, ensure children have read Chapters 4 and 5 independently.

Session 3 (Chapters 4 and 5)

> Before reading

- Recall and discuss what happened in Chapters 4 and 5. **(recall)**
- What did the children think of the new character, Colin? **(personal response)**
- How does Mary continue to change throughout these chapters?

> During reading

- Reread Chapters 4 and 5 independently, focussing particularly on Mary's relationship with Colin; compare it to her relationship with Dickon.
- Also find out as much as possible about Mr Craven, and his relationship with Colin.

> After reading

Returning to the text

Ask the children:

- What is shocking about pages 20–21? What is your reaction to Colin's circumstances?
- How does Colin respond to Mary's appearance? And what does the final panel on page 21 tell us? **(inferring)**
- Why does Mary eventually decide to tell Colin about the outdoors (p.22)? Why does she hold back on revealing the secret garden?
- What prompts Mary to reveal the secret garden to Colin on page 24?
- What are the similarities between the ways in which Colin and Mary transform through their experience of nature (p.26 in particular)? **(deducing)**
- What secret is Martha asked to keep on page 27? Why is this a dilemma for her?
- Why does Mr Craven spend time away from home? And why does he hurry back this time? **(deducing)**
- How does Mr Craven react to his newly-active son and to the children's access to his late wife's garden? Is this what we would predict?

> **Assessment point**
> Can the children discuss how a text may affect the reader and refer back to the text to back up a point of view? (ORCS Standard 6, 13)

> **Assessment point**
> Can the children read between the lines, using clues from action, dialogue and description to interpret meaning and explain how and why characters are acting, thinking or feeling? (ORCS Standard 6, 18)

Developing deeper comprehension

- How does the coming of spring reflect the development of the characters and the mood of the story? **(deducing)**
- What does this story suggest to us about the effects of keeping secrets and hiding from things on people's happiness?
- What does it have to say to us about the importance of spending time outdoors and sharing time with others? **(drawing conclusions)**
- Ask the children to look back at their completed *Changes in Mary* Photocopy Master. What events or people brought about the changes in Mary? How much was she responsible for herself?

Developing grammar, punctuation and spelling

- Write the words *through* and *bought* on the board. Ask the children what these words have in common. Now ask them to say these words. Remind them that the letter-string 'ough' can be pronounced in several different ways.

Follow-up

Writing activities

- What would Mr Craven write in his diary after the final page of this book? **(short writing task)**
- Create a leaflet promoting the beneficial effects of spending time outdoors. Make sure you include: benefits to our health and well-being; types of outdoor activity; where to visit in the local area. **(longer writing task)**

Other literacy activities

- Create freeze-frames of Mary and Colin at key points in the story or a freeze-frame of Mr Craven meeting the children in the garden on his return. In each case, use mini-whiteboards as speech or thought bubbles for your freeze-frame.

Cross-curricular activities

- Find out more about the conditions needed for plants to thrive. **(Science)**
- Design a secret garden that you would like to explore with friends. **(Art and Design)**

I Wandered Lonely as a Cloud *and other poems*

BY WILLIAM WORDSWORTH,
ROBERT LOUIS STEVENSON, WALT WHITMAN,
EMILY BRONTË AND SARA TEASDALE

Curricular correlation

English National Curriculum

Spoken language	Use relevant strategies to build their vocabulary
Word reading	Apply their growing knowledge of root words, prefixes and suffixes (etymology and morphology), both to read aloud and to understand the meaning of new words they meet
Comprehension	Identify and discuss themes and conventions in and across a wide range of writing
	Learn a wider range of poetry by heart
	Prepare poems and plays to read aloud and to perform, showing understanding through intonation, tone and volume so that the meaning is clear to an audience
	Identify how language, structure and presentation contribute to meaning
	Discuss and evaluate how authors use language, including figurative language, considering the impact on the reader

Developing grammar, punctuation and spelling

Grammar and Punctuation	Brackets, dashes or commas to indicate parenthesis	Where shall we adventure, to-day that we're afloat, Wary of the weather and steering by a star? Shall it be to Africa, a-steering of the boat, To Providence, or Babylon or off to Malabar?
Vocabulary and Spelling	Homophones and other words that are often confused	past (passed), heard (herd), father (farther)
	Challenge and context words	vales, host, continuous, margin, bay, sprightly, glee, jocund, wealth, oft, pensive, inward, bliss, solitude, picturesque, meadow, abroad, lea, wary, hi, squadron, wicket, brine, vast, lichens, turf, gluten, aliment, sluggish, suspended, disporting, flukes, leaden-eyed, pursuits, thence, subtle, sphere, siblings, thee, spray, mount, infinity, governess, initially

Reading assessment points (Oxford Reading Criterion Scale: Assessment Standard 6)

2.	Can the children clarify the meaning of unknown words from the way they are used in context? (D)
8.	Can the children use inference and deduction skills to discuss messages, moods, feelings and attitudes using the clues from the text? (D)

13.	Can the children discuss how a text may affect the reader and refer back to the text to back up a point of view? (E)
14.	Can the children identify and discuss where figurative language creates images? (E)
20.	Can the children compare and discuss different texts to discover how they are similar and how they differ in terms of character, setting, plot, structure and themes? (E/A)
21.	Can the children justify preferences in terms of authors' styles and themes? (E)
23.	Can the children identify why a long-established novel, poem or play may have retained its lasting appeal? (E)
24.	Can the children discuss the difference between literal and figurative language and the effects on imagery?

Scottish Curriculum for Excellence

Listening and talking	When listening and talking with others for different purposes, I can share information, experiences and opinions LIT 2-09a
Reading	Through developing my knowledge of context clues, punctuation, grammar and layout, I can read unfamiliar texts with increasing fluency, understanding and expression ENG 2-12a / ENG 3-12a / ENG 4-12a
	To show my understanding across different areas of learning, I can identify and consider the purpose and main ideas of a text and use supporting detail LIT 2-16a
	I can discuss structure, characterisation and/or setting; recognise the relevance of the writer's theme and how this relates to my own and others' experiences; discuss the writer's style and other features appropriate to genre ENG 2-19a

Programme of Study for English in Wales

Oracy	Listen to others, asking questions and responding to both the content and the speakers' viewpoints
Reading	Identify how punctuation relates to sentence structure and how meaning is constructed in complex sentences
	Infer meaning which is not explicitly stated, e.g. *What happens next?*, *Why did he/she do that?*
	Identify what the writer thinks about the topic, e.g. *admires a historical figure, only interested in facts*

Northern Ireland Curriculum

Talking and listening	Listen and respond to a range of fiction, poetry, drama and media texts through the use of traditional and digital resources
Reading	Extend the range of their reading and develop their own preferences
	Use a variety of reading skills for different reading purposes

Session 1 (I Wandered Lonely as a Cloud, The Wind and Pirate Story)

About this book

This is a collection of poetry inspired by nature, from five renowned poets, writing between the late 18th and early 20th centuries. It includes: 'I Wandered Lonely as a Cloud' by William Wordsworth, 'The Wind', 'Pirate Story' and 'Bed in Summer' by Robert Louis Stevenson, 'The World Below the Brine' by Walt Whitman, 'Past, Present, Future' by Emily Brontë and 'The Falling Star' by Sara Teasdale.

You will need

- *Past, Present, Future* Photocopy Master, *Graphic Texts Teaching Handbook Years 4–6* (P5–7)

Before reading

- Look together at the names in the contents, and ask the children if they have heard of any of these poets. **(building prior knowledge)**
- Explain that these poets were each inspired by aspects of nature that we may still encounter in the modern world, so the poems may well be just as meaningful to readers today.
- Some of the vocabulary, particularly in 'I Wandered Lonely as a Cloud', is quite challenging. Explain to the children that they don't need to understand every word in order to enjoy the poems, and that they can use context clues such as the meaning of surrounding words to help them work out the meanings of words they don't know. Encourage children to find interesting words in the poems as they read, and give them time to discuss the meanings or check them in a dictionary. You may also wish to read the poems aloud to the children before they start to read independently – this will give them a sense of the meaning before they begin.

Assessment point

Can the children clarify the meaning of unknown words from the way they are used in context? (ORCS Standard 6, 2)

During reading

- Ask the children to read the first three poems (up to and including p.15) independently.
- When they are reading 'I Wandered Lonely as a Cloud', ask them to try to picture what the poet is seeing (with the help of the illustrations) and how it makes him feel. **(visualizing)**
- When they are reading 'The Wind', ask them to think about their own experiences of being out in a strong wind.

- When they are reading 'Pirate Story', ask them to concentrate on what is really happening.

After reading

Returning to the text

Ask the children:

- Can they describe the actual events of Wordsworth's poem? Where is he? **(summarizing)**
- What does he compare the daffodils to and why?
- What is the overall feeling that the daffodils give him?
- In 'The Wind', who is Stevenson talking to?
- What is the poet asking and wondering throughout this poem? **(deducing)**
- What characteristics does the poet observe in the wind?
- How does 'The Wind' compare to your own experiences of a strong wind? **(empathizing)**
- Where are the children throughout 'Pirate Story'?
- What kind of adventure do they go on? What is actually happening?

Developing deeper comprehension

- Looking back at 'I Wandered Lonely as a Cloud', what can we say Wordsworth gets out of being in nature? **(inferring)**
- What is the *wealth* he mentions on page 4? When does he actually experience this wealth (p.5)?
- Find examples of personification throughout Wordsworth's poem and explain why each has been chosen.
- How does he feel about being alone? How does the personification of the daffodils appear to help him? What is meant by *jocund company* and how are the daffodils like this?
- The illustrator has given the character a modern phone on which to look at the daffodils; compare this to Wordsworth's experience in the early 19th century.
- In 'The Wind', why does the poet imagine that there is a being of some kind behind the actions?

Assessment point

Can the children identify and discuss where figurative language creates images? (ORCS Standard 6, 14)

Developing deeper comprehension continued

- What is particularly mysterious about the wind, according to Stevenson?
- Is there any judgement made about what the wind gets up to?
- Why does he wonder if the wind is a beast, or a strong child?
- In 'Pirate Story', what provokes the children to imagine they are on the ocean?
- What have the three poems got in common?

Assessment point
Can the children compare and discuss different texts to discover how they are similar and how they differ in terms of character, setting, plot, structure and themes? (ORCS Standard 6, 20)

Developing grammar, punctuation and spelling

- Turn to the text-only version of 'Pirate Story' (p.15), and ask the children to find two examples of commas used for parenthesis in the middle stanza, *Where shall we adventure, to-day that we're afloat, wary of the weather* and *Shall it be to Africa, a-steering of the boat, To Providence, or Babylon, or off to Malabar*.
- Ask them which other punctuation marks could have been used for a similar effect, e.g. brackets or dashes, and rewrite the stanza using these marks to confirm this.

- Prior to Session 2, ensure children have read the rest of the poems in the collection, independently.

Session 2 (Bed in Summer, The World Below the Brine, Past, Present, Future and The Falling Star)

❯ Before reading
- Introduce the session by turning to page 24 and reading 'The World Below the Brine' out loud to the children. Encourage them to listen with closed eyes and try to picture the world described in the poem.
- Discuss their impressions of the poem – did they enjoy it? Which parts did they particularly like or dislike? Explain that it's not essential to understand every word to enjoy a poem like this, but help them to understand any parts they found confusing, by looking up words as necessary in a dictionary.

❯ During reading
Allocate each child a different poem to read independently.
- Those reading 'Bed in Summer' (p.16–18) should think about what the poet's complaint is and whether they agree with him.
- Those reading 'The World Below the Brine' (p.20–24) should think about how the poet describes the living things in the poem.
- Those reading 'Past, Present, Future' (p.26–29) should think about the child's attitude to the passing of time.
- Those reading 'The Falling Star' (p.31–32) should imagine what they would feel if they were the observer in the poem. Ask these children to choose another poem to read when they have finished.

❯ After reading
Returning to the text
Ask the children:
- In 'Bed in Summer', can you find examples where the poet is calling on the senses of sight and hearing? Why do you think he emphasizes the senses?
- Can you read 'Bed in Summer' out loud so that it really sounds like a child complaining?
- Which different aspects of the ocean are described in 'The World Below the Brine' on pages 20–22?
- What is your favourite line in 'The World Below the Brine' and why?
- What do you think of the way this poem is illustrated? Do the illustrations help convey the mood of the poem? In what way? **(visualizing)**
- How is 'Past, Present, Future' structured, in words and illustrations?
- What is the mood throughout the poem? How do you know?
- In 'The Falling Star', what is being observed? What is it good for?

Assessment point
Can the children discuss the difference between literal and figurative language and the effects on imagery? (ORCS Standard 6, 24)

> **Developing deeper comprehension**

- How has the illustrator changed perspective over the first three panels on page 20? Why? (**visualizing**, **deducing**)
- How does the perspective change from the middle of page 23? What does this tell us about Whitman's wondering? **(drawing conclusions)**
- What makes Whitman wonder about the experience of beings on other worlds?
- In 'Past, Present, Future', how does the illustrator show the passing of time? **(visualizing)**
- What metaphors/similes have been used by the child? Why did Brontë choose these analogies?
- Which language choices influence the mood of each page?
- What is the child's attitude to her future? How has the illustrator reinforced this?
- Using the *Past, Present, Future* Photocopy Master, write your own answers to the older lady's questions. Try to use metaphors/similes, as Emily Brontë does.
- In 'The Falling Star', which words emphasize the fact that the star is unattainable? What is the effect of the repeated *too*?
- What attributes make the falling star seem special? Ensure its temporary nature is understood. **(deducing)**

Assessment point

Can the children use inference and deduction skills to discuss messages, moods, feelings and attitudes using the clues from the text? (ORCS Standard 6, 8)

- Prior to Session 3, ensure children revisit the entire book independently.

Session 3 (whole book)

Before reading
- Now that the whole text has been read at least twice, ask the children if they have noticed any common themes throughout.
- Discuss preferences; do they have a favourite from the collection? Why? **(personal response)**
- Ask them if they have read the original, text-only versions of the poems, and if they have any thoughts on the contrasts between the versions.

During reading
- Ask the children to revisit the entire book, trying to notice common themes and attitudes.

After reading
Returning to the text

Ask the children:
- Which poem meant the most to them, and why? **(personal response)**
- Which poem was the most challenging to access, and what strategies did they use to get meaning from it?
- In what ways do the illustrations add to the poems? Are there any instances where the illustrations detract from the poetry?
- Why do you think these poems are still popular? In what ways have the illustrations been used to make these 19th century poems accessible to 21st century readers? **(visualization, deducing)**
- Encourage the children to choose their favourite poem and, working in pairs or small groups, expain to others why they chose their poem, referring to the style it's written in and/or the themes it covers. **(personal response)**

> **Assessment point**
> Can the children discuss how a text may affect the reader and refer back to the text to back up a point of view? (ORCS Standard 6, 13)

> **Assessment point**
> Can the children identify why a long-established novel, poem or play may have retained its lasting appeal? (ORCS Standard 6, 23)

> **Assessment point**
> Can the children justify preferences in terms of authors' styles and themes? (ORCS Standard 6, 21)

Developing deeper comprehension

- Taking each poem in turn, discuss how imagination is applied to nature. How does nature inspire imagination?
- Are there any reasons for reading the text-only versions of the poems first? Which way round would you recommend to other readers of this book?
- Which poem is the most reflective? Which is the most imaginative? Evidence must be used for each justification. **(drawing conclusions)**

Developing grammar, punctuation and spelling

- Ask the group to scan back through the book and see if they can spot any homophones, for example *past* (p.17), *heard* (p.9) and *father* (p.19). Discuss how important it is to choose the correct spelling of the word you mean so as not to cause confusion. Ask them to write sentences using the wrong homophone and explain the change in meaning, e.g. *Still going passed me in the street.*

Follow-up

Writing activities

- Try writing a personification poem like 'The Wind', but about another form of weather, for example, the rain, the sunshine, snow or a rainbow. **(longer writing task)**

Other literacy activities

- Working as a pair or in a small group, practise reading your favourite poem aloud for a performance. You may want to learn all or part of your chosen poem by heart.

Cross-curricular activities

- Research the sea creatures mentioned in 'The World Below the Brine'. Draw the creatures and describe their habitats and behaviours. **(Science/Geography)**

Great Naturalists

BY JAMES DRIVER

Curricular correlation

English National Curriculum

Spoken language	Give well-structured descriptions, explanations and narratives for different purposes, including for expressing feelings
Word reading	Apply their growing knowledge of root words, prefixes and suffixes (etymology and morphology), both to read aloud and to understand the meaning of new words they meet
Comprehension	Make comparisons within and across books
	Ask questions to improve their understanding
	Summarise the main ideas drawn from more than one paragraph, identifying key details that support the main ideas
	Retrieve, record and present information from non-fiction

Developing grammar, punctuation and spelling

Grammar and Punctuation	**Relative clauses** beginning with *who*, *which*, *where*, *when*, *whose*, *that*, or an omitted relative pronoun	when, who, which, where
Vocabulary and Spelling	Words with 'silent' letters	islands, know, wrote, knew, honeycomb, writes
	Challenge and context words	species, evolved, argumentative, conservation, habitats, rumoured, settlers, expeditions, pollinate, nectar, antennae, honeycomb, waggle, physiology, zoology, institute, palaeontologist, landslide, fossilized, extinct, Geological Society, spores, memorial, dedicated, fellow, biodiversity, generations

Reading assessment points (Oxford Reading Criterion Scale: Assessment Standard 6)

6. Can the children summarize and explain the main points in a text, referring back to the text to support and clarify summaries? (R)
9. Can the children identify the point of view from which a story is told? (D)
11. Can the children discuss how an author builds a character through dialogue, action and description? (D)
13. Can the children discuss how a text may affect the reader and refer back to the text to back up a point of view? (E)
16. Can the children infer and deduce meaning based on evidence drawn from different points in the text? (D)
18. Can the children read between the lines, using clues from action, dialogue and description to interpret meaning and explain how and why characters are acting, thinking or feeling? (D)

Scottish Curriculum for Excellence

Listening and talking	I can select ideas and relevant information, organise these in an appropriate way for my purpose and use suitable vocabulary for my audience LIT 2-06a
Reading	Using what I know about the features of different types of texts, I can find, select and sort information from a variety of sources and use this for different purposes LIT 2-14a
	To show my understanding across different areas of learning, I can identify and consider the purpose and main ideas of a text and use supporting detail LIT 2-16a
	To show my understanding, I can respond to literal, inferential and evaluative questions and other close reading tasks and can create different kinds of questions of my own ENG 2-17a

Programme of Study for English in Wales

Oracy	Explain information and ideas, exploring and using ways to be convincing, *e.g. use of vocabulary, gesture, visual aids*
Reading	Scan to find specific details using graphic and textual organisers, *e.g. sub-headings, diagrams*
	Identify and explore ideas and information that interest them
	Gather and organise information and ideas from different sources

Northern Ireland Curriculum

Talking and listening	Read aloud, inflecting appropriately, to express thoughts and feelings and emphasise the meaning of what they have read, for example, talk about an idea they have
Reading	Consider, interpret and discuss texts, exploring the ways in which language can be manipulated in order to affect the reader or engage attention
	Use a range of cross-checking strategies to read unfamiliar words in texts

Session 1 (pages 2–14)

> **About this book**
> This graphic text presents biographical summaries of seven important naturalists (Jane Goodall, John James Audubon, Karl von Frisch, Mary Anning, Kathleen Drew-Baker and David Douglas), explaining how their research has impacted on our knowledge of the natural world.
>
> **You will need**
> - *Nobel Prize* Photocopy Master, *Graphic Texts Teaching Handbook Years 4–6 (P5–7)*

Before reading

- Introduce the term 'naturalist' and see if any of the children have heard of Charles Darwin or Jane Goodall (or any other naturalist). **(activating prior knowledge)**
- Explain that this book presents briefly the key work of seven naturalists, and it may be that it inspires further research.

During reading

- Ask the children to read the first three chapters, up to and including page 14, independently.
- Ask that they try to remember what each of the three naturalists is best known for and what difference their studies may have made. They could also think about what the three have in common.
- Also ask the children to look out for words with silent letters, e.g. *islands*, *know* (p.2), as they read.

After reading

Returning to the text

Challenge the children to attempt to answer these questions with closed books; they may of course quickly reread if necessary:

- What did Darwin do in the Galapagos islands, and when?
- Why did he record the information?
- What are the key things Darwin says a naturalist must do?
- What is Jane Goodall's expertise?
- How did she become interested in animals?
- Where did she travel to?
- How did she get the chimpanzees to trust her?

Great Naturalists

- What things previously thought to be unique to humans did she find that chimpanzees could do?
- What did Goodall subsequently make her life's work?
- What was Audubon's passion?
- Why was he an unsuccessful shopkeeper?
- What did his wife do to support his work?
- Why did he have to start all of his drawings again?
- Where did he go to become a success, and why?

⇒ Developing deeper comprehension

- What is significant about what Darwin says about the shell in the second frame on page 2? **(deducing)**
- Why has the author decided to begin the book with Darwin, and who is he speaking to in the final frame on page 3? What is the overall purpose of page 3?
- Which characteristics made Goodall a great naturalist, even from an early age? **(inferring)**
- What was the significance of finding that chimpanzees were capable of doing things that it was previously believed only humans could do?
- Why does the Audubon chapter begin in 2010, with the information about the price of his book? Ensure the children understand the contrast with his poverty and struggle.
- How did Audubon feel when the rats ate his artwork (p. 11)? Why might it be seen as good fortune in the long run? **(empathizing, deducing)**
- What part did his wife Lucy play in his eventual success? Why do you think she helped him so much?
- At which points in this story does Audubon show resilience?

Assessment point
Can the children identify the point of view from which a story is told? (ORCS Standard 6, 9)

Assessment point
Can the children discuss how an author builds a character through dialogue, action and description? (ORCS Standard 6, 11)

> *Developing grammar, punctuation and spelling*
> - Ask the children to share the words they found with silent letters, e.g. *islands*, *know*. Together, try to think of different ways to remember them.
> - Ask them to look out for further examples as they continue to read through the book.

- Prior to Session 2, ensure children have read pages 15–29 independently.

Session 2 (pages 15–29)

Before reading
- Begin by recapping as much as possible from the independent reading of the last four naturalists.
- Did the four have any characteristics in common? What makes each of them special? **(recall)**

During reading
- Ask the children to reread pages 15–29 independently, focussing on the key aspects of their work.
- Ask them also to be ready to talk about their characteristics.

After reading
Returning to the text

Challenge the children again to answer these questions with closed books; they may of course quickly reread if necessary:
- When and where did von Frisch do his most significant work?
- What is extraordinary about his discovery?
- What is the reaction to his discovery (p.16)?
- How did he enable the observation of bees within their hive?
- What can you recall of how bees communicate?
- When and where did Mary Anning live and work?
- What is a palaeontologist?
- What 'firsts' did Mary Anning achieve?
- Why was her work not officially recognized?

Great Naturalists

- When and where did Kathleen Drew-Baker work?
- What was her discovery, and why was it so important to people in Japan?
- In which two countries do we know David Douglas spent time? And when was this?
- What did he do, and why was it important?

Developing deeper comprehension

- On page 15, what is implied about von Frisch's motivation? Why is the year and the country significant? **(inferring, deducing)**
- Contrast the reaction he gets on page 16, with the last panel on page 19; what has happened in the intervening years? **(deducing)**
- How do we know that Mary Anning is brave and resilient? (See page 21 and the information on page 25.)
- What does the speech bubble in the second panel on page 24 tell us about Britain at this time? How are things different now?
- Why was a memorial dedicated to Kathleen Drew-Baker?
- What does Drew-Baker's story tell us about the importance of specialist studies and careful hard work, even when the subject matter seems unexciting? **(drawing conclusions)**
- How did Douglas change the lives of British people? Give detailed evidence.

Assessment point
Can the children infer and deduce meaning based on evidence drawn from different points in the text? (ORCS Standard 6, 16)

Assessment point
Can the children summarize and explain the main points in a text, referring back to the text to support and clarify summaries? (ORCS Standard 6, 6)

> **Developing grammar, punctuation and spelling**
>
> - Turn to page 15 and read the text in frame 7 together (*In return, the bees pollinate the plants, which make the seeds and fruit we eat.*)
> - Discuss the use of the word 'which' and that it is used to link two parts of the sentence together.

- Prior to Session 3, ensure children have reread all of the previous sections, as well as reading the final section (p. 30–31) independently.

Session 3 (pages 30–31)

Before reading

- Together, summarize what has been learnt so far about naturalists. **(summarizing)**
- What individual contributions can be recalled? **(recall)**
- Which characteristics could we say they share?

During reading

- Ask the children to reread 'Naturalists today' independently.
- What reason does this spread give for saying that we need naturalists more than ever?
- How do the author and illustrator work together in this section to make the job of a naturalist seem appealing? **(drawing conclusions)**

After reading

Returning to the text

Ask the children:

- Why do we need naturalists in the 21st century, according to this section?
- What is the most important characteristic of a naturalist, according to the author?
- Which famous naturalist have we returned to in this chapter? Why? **(deducing)**
- What might inspire readers of this final chapter to become naturalists?

> **Assessment point**
> Can the children discuss how a text may affect the reader and refer back to the text to back up a point of view? (ORCS Standard 6, 13)

Developing deeper comprehension

- Ask the children to work in pairs to skim-read the entire book and find examples of the great naturalists showing curiosity. Discuss each of these examples, and ensure that there is understanding of the importance of wondering throughout.
- Similarly, return to the text and find examples of resilience. Discuss these examples, and talk about why this is also an important trait for a naturalist.

Assessment point
Can the children read between the lines, using clues from action, dialogue and description to interpret meaning and explain how and why characters are acting, thinking or feeling? (ORCS Standard 6, 18)

Follow-up

Writing activities

- Use the *Nobel Prize* Photocopy Master to make notes on the key work of two of the naturalists from the book. Through discussion with friends, decide which naturalist you would award a Nobel prize to, and why. (**short writing task**)
- Write a job description or advert for a 21st-century naturalist. (**longer writing task**)

Other literacy activities

- Prepare a presentation or display explaining, with detailed examples, how bees communicate via dance.

Cross-curricular activities

- Further research the behaviour of bees or chimpanzees. (**Science/Geography**)
- Choose one of the naturalists to study in more detail. (**Science**)